Filet Afghans

Filet crochet isn't just for doilies anymore! These eight charted designs for afghans finish quickly, with pretty images of birds in flight, easy geometrics, a delicate butterfly, or Art Deco florals. You'll race through the rows of simple stitches, adding the lacy look of filet crochet to your home in a bold new way—with an afghan for every room!

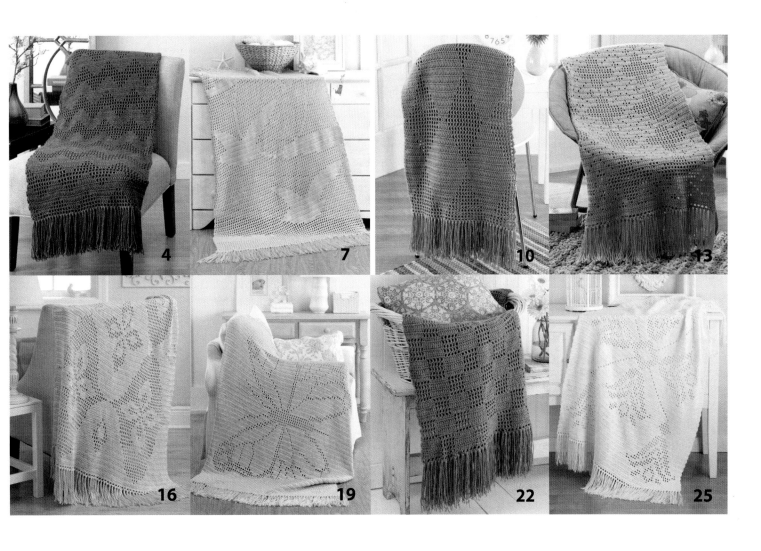

LEISURE ARTS, INC. • Maumelle, Arkansas

Introduction to Filet Crochet

Filet crochet is a decorative design technique in which pictures, motifs, or patterns are created by combining solid and open-space blocks. Each solid and open-space block is a combination of two stitches: chain stitches and double crochets.

Most often, filet crochet is worked from a square-grid chart, which greatly simplifies the instructions to complete a pattern. Listed below are all of the combinations of solid and open-space blocks necessary to complete any of the afghans in this leaflet.

Basic Chart Stitches

Beginning Block Over Space
Ch 3 (**does not count as a stitch**), turn; dc in first dc and in next ch, dc in next dc.

Beginning Space Over Space
Ch 3 (**does not count as a stitch**), turn; dc in first dc, ch 1, dc in next dc.

Beginning Block Over Block
Ch 3 (**does not count as a stitch**), turn; dc in first 3 dc.

Beginning Space Over Block
Ch 3 (**does not count as a stitch**), turn; dc in first dc, ch 1, skip next dc, dc in next dc.

Block Over Space
Dc in next ch and in next dc.

Space Over Space
Ch 1, dc in next dc.

Block Over Block
Dc in next 2 dc.

Space Over Block
Ch 1, skip next dc, dc in next dc.

Sample Chart

The Sample Chart, right, includes all of the Basic Chart Stitches. Successfully completing the Sample Chart will enable you to create any of the afghans included in this leaflet.

Ch 12.

Row 1 (Right side)**:** Dc in fourth ch from hook **(3 skipped chs do not count as a stitch)**, (ch 1, skip next ch, dc in next ch) across: 4 ch-1 sps.

Loop a short piece of yarn through any stitch to mark Row 1 as **right** side.

Row 2: Work Beginning Space Over Space, work Space Over Space, work Block Over Space twice.

Row 3: Work Beginning Space Over Block, work Space Over Block, work Block Over Space twice.

Row 4: Work Beginning Block Over Block, work Block Over Block, work Space Over Space twice.

Row 5: Work Beginning Block Over Space, work Block Over Space, work Block Over Block twice; finish off.

Once familiar with the variations of Blocks and Spaces, the instructions for Rows 2-5 can be further condensed as follows:

Rows 2-5: Follow Chart.

Finish off.

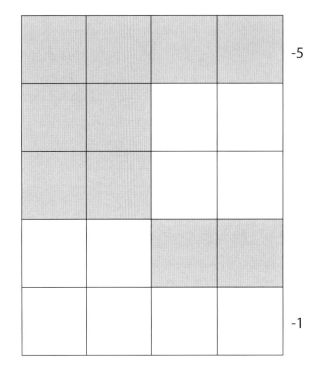

KEY

□ 1 Block = 2 dc

□ 1 Space = ch 1, dc

It is important to note the **right** side of your piece as labeled in the instructions. This will help you determine from which direction to follow the chart. On **right** side rows, work chart from **right** to **left**; on **wrong** side rows, work chart from **left** to **right**.

Mulberry Ripple

■■□□ **EASY**

Finished Size: 41" w x 56" l, excluding fringe (104 cm x 142 cm)

MATERIALS
Medium Weight Yarn
    [5 ounces, 249 yards
    (142 grams, 227 meters) per skein]: 8 skeins
Crochet hook, size J (6 mm) **or** size needed for gauge
Yarn needle

GAUGE: 16 dc and 8 rows = 4" (10 cm)

Gauge Swatch: 4" square (10 cm)
Ch 19.
Row 1: Dc in fourth ch from hook and in each
ch across **(3 skipped chs do not count as a stitch)**.
Rows 2-8: Ch 3 **(does not count as a stitch, now
and throughout)**, turn; dc in each dc across: 16 dc.
Finish off.

Refer to Basic Chart Stitches, page 2.

AFGHAN

Ch 164.

Row 1 (Wrong side)**:** Dc in fourth ch from hook
(3 skipped chs do not count as a stitch), (ch 1, skip
next ch, dc in next ch) across: 80 ch-1 sps.

Loop a short piece of yarn through back of any stitch
to mark **right** side.

Rows 2-111: Follow Chart, page 6.

Finish off.

FINISHING

Add fringe in each ch-1 sp across short edges of
Afghan *(Figs. 1a & b, page 29)*.

Chart shown on Page 6

On **right** side rows, work chart from **right** to **left**;
On **wrong** side rows, work chart from **left** to **right**.

KEY
■ 1 Block = 2dc
□ 1 Space = ch1, dc

Blue Seagull Fantasy

 **EASY**

Finished Size: 37" w x 48½" l, excluding fringe (94 cm x 123 cm)

MATERIALS
Medium Weight Yarn **4 MEDIUM**
   [6 ounces, 315 yards
   (170 grams, 288 meters) per skein]: 5 skeins
Crochet hook, size J (6 mm) **or** size needed for gauge
Yarn needle

GAUGE: 16 dc and 8 rows = 4" (10 cm)

Gauge Swatch: 4" square (10 cm)
Ch 19.
Row 1: Dc in fourth ch from hook and in each
ch across (**3 skipped chs do not count as a stitch**).
Rows 2-8: Ch 3 (**does not count as a stitch, now and
throughout**), turn; dc in each dc across: 16 dc.
Finish off.

Refer to Basic Chart Stitches, page 2.

AFGHAN
Ch 152.

Row 1 (Right side)**:** Dc in fourth ch from hook
(**3 skipped chs do not count as a stitch**), (ch 1, skip
next ch, dc in next ch) across: 74 ch-1 sps.

Loop a short piece of yarn through any stitch to mark
Row 1 as **right** side.

Rows 2-97: Follow Chart, page 8.

Finish off.

FINISHING
Add fringe in each ch-1 sp across short edges of
Afghan *(Figs. 1a & b, page 29)*.

Chart shown on Page 8

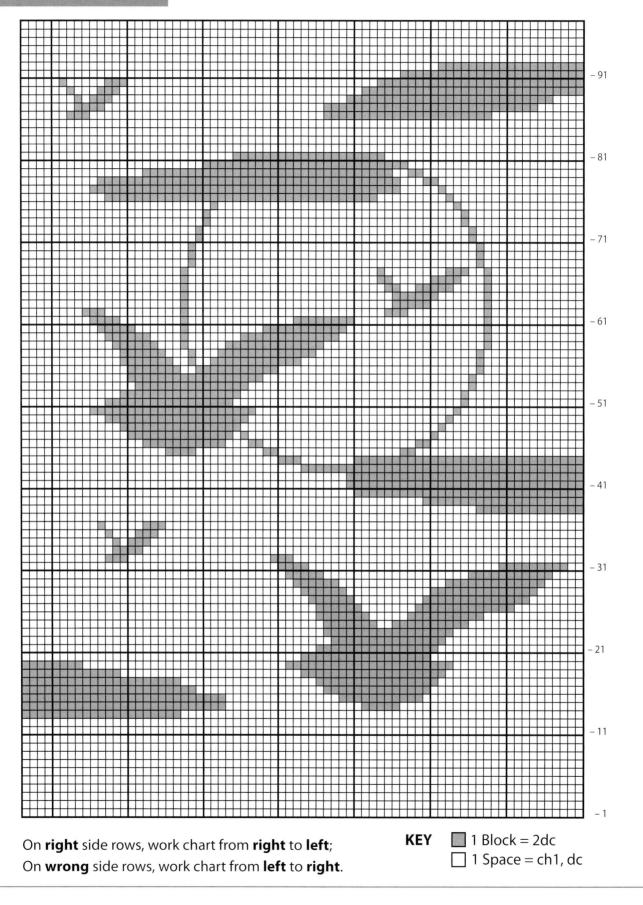

On **right** side rows, work chart from **right** to **left**;
On **wrong** side rows, work chart from **left** to **right**.

KEY
- 1 Block = 2dc
- 1 Space = ch1, dc

Blueberry Diamonds

 EASY

Finished Size: 37" w x 55" l, excluding fringe (94 cm x 139.5 cm)

MATERIALS
Medium Weight Yarn 4
   [5 ounces, 249 yards
   (142 grams, 227 meters) per skein]: 7 skeins
Crochet hook, size J (6 mm) **or** size needed for gauge
Yarn needle

GAUGE: 16 dc and 8 rows = 4" (10 cm)

Gauge Swatch: 4" square (10 cm)
Ch 19.
Row 1: Dc in fourth ch from hook and in each
ch across **(3 skipped chs do not count as a stitch)**.
Rows 2-8: Ch 3 **(does not count as a stitch, now and
throughout)**, turn; dc in each dc across: 16 dc.
Finish off.

Refer to Basic Chart Stitches, page 2.

AFGHAN
Ch 150.

Row 1 (Right side)**:** Dc in fourth ch from hook
(3 skipped chs do not count as a stitch), (ch 1, skip
next ch, dc in next ch) across: 73 ch-1 sps.

Loop a short piece of yarn through any stitch to mark
Row 1 as **right** side.

Rows 2-109: Follow Chart, page 12.

Finish off.

FINISHING
Add fringe in each ch-1 sp across short edges of
Afghan *(Figs. 1a & b, page 29)*.

Chart shown on Page 12

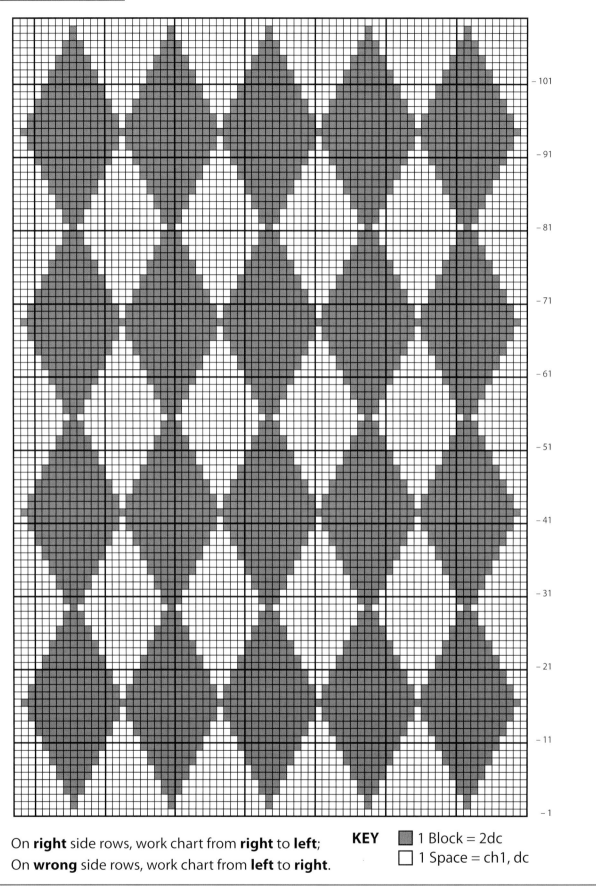

— 101

— 91

— 81

— 71

— 61

— 51

— 41

— 31

— 21

— 11

— 1

On **right** side rows, work chart from **right** to **left**;
On **wrong** side rows, work chart from **left** to **right**.

KEY

■ 1 Block = 2dc
□ 1 Space = ch1, dc

Lilac Mosaic

Finished Size: 35" w x 52" l, excluding fringe (89 cm x 132 cm)

MATERIALS
Medium Weight Yarn **4**
[5 ounces, 249 yards
(142 grams, 227 meters) per skein]: 8 skeins
Crochet hook, size J (6 mm) **or** size needed for gauge
Yarn needle

GAUGE: 16 dc and 8 rows = 4" (10 cm)

Gauge Swatch: 4" square (10 cm)
Ch 19.
Row 1: Dc in fourth ch from hook and in each
ch across **(3 skipped chs do not count as a stitch)**.
Rows 2-8: Ch 3 **(does not count as a stitch, now and
throughout)**, turn; dc in each dc across: 16 dc.
Finish off.

Refer to Basic Chart Stitches, page 2.

AFGHAN
Ch 142.

Row 1 (Wrong side)**:** Dc in fourth ch from hook
(3 skipped chs do not count as a stitch), (ch 1, skip
next ch, dc in next ch) across: 69 ch-1 sps.

Loop a short piece of yarn through back of any stitch
to mark **right** side.

Rows 2-103: Follow Chart, page 14.

Finish off.

FINISHING
Add fringe in each ch-1 sp across short edges of
Afghan *(Figs. 1a & b, page 29)*.

Chart shown on Page 14

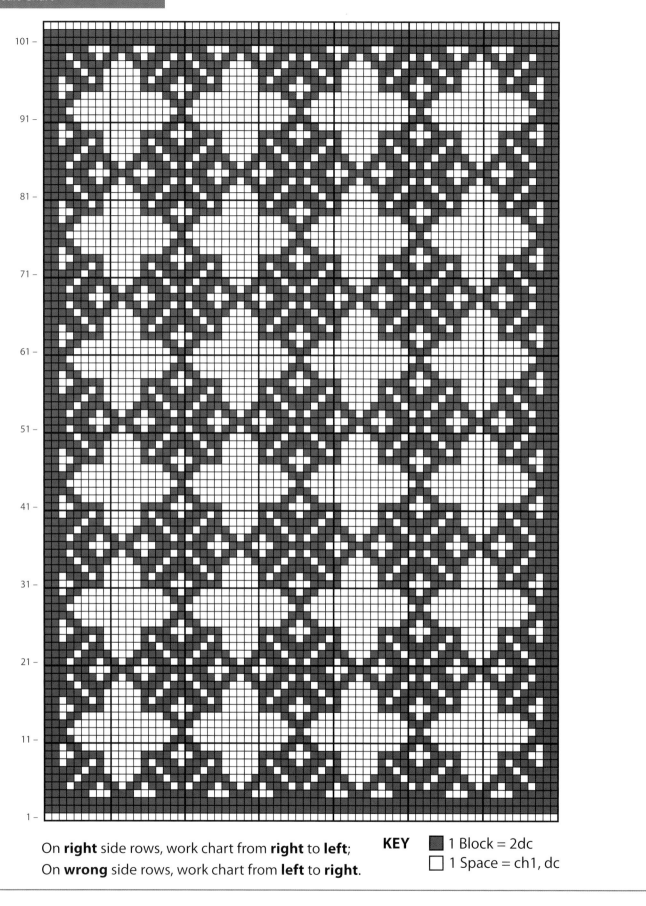

On **right** side rows, work chart from **right** to **left**;
On **wrong** side rows, work chart from **left** to **right**.

KEY
■ 1 Block = 2dc
□ 1 Space = ch1, dc

Peach Opposites Attract

 **EASY**

Finished Size: 37" w x 52" l, excluding fringe (94 cm x 129.5 cm)

MATERIALS
Medium Weight Yarn **4**
[6 ounces, 315 yards
(170 grams, 288 meters) per skein]: 5 skeins
Crochet hook, size J (6 mm) **or** size needed for gauge
Yarn needle

GAUGE: 16 dc and 8 rows = 4" (10 cm)

Gauge Swatch: 4" square (10 cm)
Ch 19.
Row 1: Dc in fourth ch from hook and in each
ch across (**3 skipped chs do not count as a stitch**).
Rows 2-8: Ch 3 (**does not count as a stitch, now and
throughout**), turn; dc in each dc across: 16 dc.
Finish off.

Refer to Basic Chart Stitches, page 2.

AFGHAN
Ch 150.

Row 1 (Wrong side)**:** Dc in fourth ch from hook
(**3 skipped chs do not count as a stitch**), (ch 1, skip
next ch, dc in next ch) across: 73 ch-1 sps.

Loop a short piece of yarn through back of any stitch
to mark **right** side.

Rows 2-101: Follow Chart, page 18.

Finish off.

FINISHING
Add fringe in each ch-1 sp across short edges of
Afghan (*Figs. 1a & b, page 29*).

Chart shown on Page 18

On **right** side rows, work chart from **right** to **left**;
On **wrong** side rows, work chart from **left** to **right**.

KEY

- ▨ 1 Block = 2dc
- ☐ 1 Space = ch1, dc

Pink Butterfly

Finished Size: 41" w x 52" l, excluding fringe (104 cm x 134.5 cm)

MATERIALS
Medium Weight Yarn
  [6 ounces, 315 yards
  (170 grams, 288 meters) per skein]: 6 skeins
Crochet hook, size J (6 mm) **or** size needed for gauge
Yarn needle

GAUGE: 16 dc and 8 rows = 4" (10 cm)

Gauge Swatch: 4" square (10 cm)
Ch 19.
Row 1: Dc in fourth ch from hook and in each
ch across (**3 skipped chs do not count as a stitch**).
Rows 2-8: Ch 3 (**does not count as a stitch, now and
throughout**), turn; dc in each dc across: 16 dc.
Finish off.

Refer to Basic Chart Stitches, page 2.

AFGHAN
Ch 164.

Row 1 (Wrong side)**:** Dc in fourth ch from hook
(**3 skipped chs do not count as a stitch**), (ch 1, skip
next ch, dc in next ch) across: 80 ch-1 sps.

Loop a short piece of yarn through back of any stitch
to mark **right** side.

Rows 2-105: Follow Chart, page 20.

Finish off.

FINISHING
Add fringe in each ch-1 sp across short edges of
Afghan (*Figs. 1a & b, page 29*).

Chart shown on Page 20

On **right** side rows, work chart from **right** to **left**;
On **wrong** side rows, work chart from **left** to **right**.

KEY
☐ 1 Block = 2dc
☐ 1 Space = ch1, dc

Grey Simply Squares

Finished Size: 38" w x 54" l, excluding fringe (96.5 cm x 137 cm)

MATERIALS
Medium Weight Yarn
   [6 ounces, 315 yards
   (170 grams, 288 meters) per skein]: 5 skeins
Crochet hook, size J (6 mm) **or** size needed for gauge
Yarn needle

GAUGE: 16 dc and 8 rows = 4" (10 cm)

Gauge Swatch: 4" square (10 cm)
Ch 19.
Row 1: Dc in fourth ch from hook and in each
ch across (**3 skipped chs do not count as a stitch**).
Rows 2-8: Ch 3 (**does not count as a stitch, now and
throughout**), turn; dc in each dc across: 16 dc.
Finish off.

Refer to Basic Chart Stitches, page 2.

AFGHAN
Ch 154.

Row 1 (Wrong side)**:** Dc in fourth ch from hook
(**3 skipped chs do not count as a stitch**), (ch 1, skip
next ch, dc in next ch) across: 75 ch-1 sps.

Loop a short piece of yarn through back of any stitch
to mark **right** side.

Rows 2-107: Follow Chart, page 24.

Finish off.

FINISHING
Add fringe in each ch-1 sp across short edges of
Afghan (*Figs. 1a & b, page 29*).

Chart shown on Page 24

On **right** side rows, work chart from **right** to **left**;
On **wrong** side rows, work chart from **left** to **right**.

KEY

■ 1 Block = 2dc
□ 1 Space = ch1, dc

Yellow Springtime

◖■▢▷ **EASY**

Finished Size: 35" w x 53" l, excluding fringe (89 cm x 134.5 cm)

MATERIALS
Medium Weight Yarn
  [6 ounces, 315 yards
  (170 grams, 288 meters) per skein]: 5 skeins
Crochet hook, size J (6 mm) **or** size needed for gauge
Yarn needle

GAUGE: 16 dc and 8 rows = 4" (10 cm)

Gauge Swatch: 4" square (10 cm)
Ch 19.
Row 1: Dc in fourth ch from hook and in each
ch across (**3 skipped chs do not count as a stitch**).
Rows 2-8: Ch 3 (**does not count as a stitch, now and
throughout**), turn; dc in each dc across: 16 dc.
Finish off.

Refer to Basic Chart Stitches, page 2.

AFGHAN
Ch 142.

Row 1 (Right side)**:** Dc in fourth ch from hook
(**3 skipped chs do not count as a stitch**), (ch 1, skip
next ch, dc in next ch) across: 69 ch-1 sps.

Loop a short piece of yarn through any stitch to mark
Row 1 as **right** side.

Rows 2-107: Follow Chart, page 26.

Finish off.

FINISHING
Add fringe in each ch-1 sp across short edges of
Afghan *(Figs. 1a & b, page 29)*.

Chart shown on Page 26

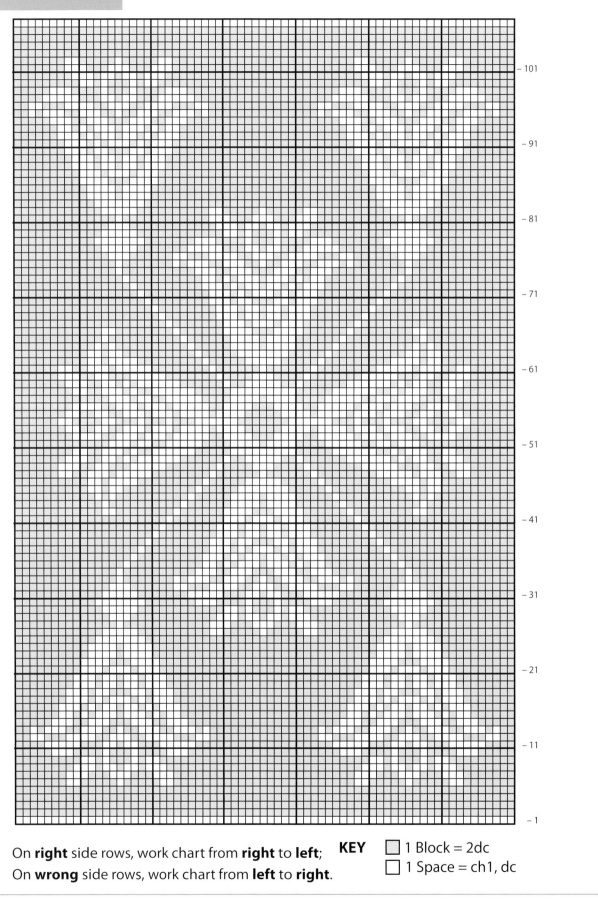

- 101
- 91
- 81
- 71
- 61
- 51
- 41
- 31
- 21
- 11
- 1

On **right** side rows, work chart from **right** to **left**;
On **wrong** side rows, work chart from **left** to **right**.

KEY

☐ 1 Block = 2dc
☐ 1 Space = ch1, dc

Abbreviations

ch(s) chain(s)
cm   centimeters
dc   double crochet(s)
mm   millimeters
sp(s) space(s)
st(s) stitch(es)

( ) or [ ] – work enclosed instructions **as many** times as specified by the number immediately following **or** contains explanatory remarks.

colon (:) – the numbers given after a colon at the end of a row or round denote the number of stitches you should have on that row or round.

CROCHET TERMINOLOGY	
UNITED STATES	INTERNATIONAL
slip stitch (slip st) =	single crochet (sc)
single crochet (sc) =	double crochet (dc)
half double crochet (hdc) =	half treble crochet (htr)
double crochet (dc) =	treble crochet (tr)
treble crochet (tr) =	double treble crochet (dtr)
double treble crochet (dtr) =	triple treble crochet (ttr)
triple treble crochet (tr tr) =	quadruple treble crochet (qtr)
skip =	miss

Yarn Weight Symbol & Names	LACE 0	SUPER FINE 1	FINE 2	LIGHT 3	MEDIUM 4	BULKY 5	SUPER BULKY 6
Type of Yarns in Category	Fingering, 10-count crochet thread	Sock, Fingering Baby	Sport, Baby	DK, Light Worsted	Worsted, Afghan, Aran	Chunky, Craft, Rug	Bulky, Roving
Crochet Gauge* Ranges in Single Crochet to 4" (10 cm)	32-42 double crochets**	21-32 sts	16-20 sts	12-17 sts	11-14 sts	8-11 sts	5-9 sts
Advised Hook Size Range	Steel*** 6,7,8 Regular hook B-1	B-1 to E-4	E-4 to 7	7 to I-9	I-9 to K-10.5	K-10.5 to M-13	M-13 and larger

*GUIDELINES ONLY: The chart above reflects the most commonly used gauges and hook sizes for specific yarn categories.

** Lace weight yarns are usually crocheted on larger-size hooks to create lacy openwork patterns. Accordingly, a gauge range is difficult to determine. Always follow the gauge stated in your pattern.

CROCHET HOOKS												
U.S.	B-1	C-2	D-3	E-4	F-5	G-6	H-8	I-9	J-10	K-10½	N	P	Q
Metric - mm	2.25	2.75	3.25	3.5	3.75	4	5	5.5	6	6.5	9	10	15

■□□□ BEGINNER	Projects for first-time crocheters using basic stitches. Minimal shaping.
■■□□ EASY	Projects using yarn with basic stitches, repetitive stitch patterns, simple color changes, and simple shaping and finishing.
■■■□ INTERMEDIATE	Projects using a variety of techniques, such as basic lace patterns or color patterns, mid-level shaping and finishing.
■■■■ EXPERIENCED	Projects with intricate stitch patterns, techniques and dimension, such as non-repeating patterns, multi-color techniques, fine threads, small hooks, detailed shaping and refined finishing.

GAUGE

Exact gauge is essential for proper size. Before beginning your project, make the sample swatch given in the individual instructions in the yarn and hook specified. After completing the swatch, measure it, counting your stitches and rows carefully. If your swatch is larger or smaller than specified, **make another, changing hook size to get the correct gauge**. Keep trying until you find the size hook that will give you the specified gauge.

HINTS

As in all crocheted pieces, good finishing techniques make a big difference in the quality of the piece. Make a habit of taking care of loose ends as you work. Thread a yarn needle with the yarn end. With **wrong** side facing, weave the needle through several stitches, then reverse the direction and weave it back through several stitches. When ends are secure, clip them off close to work.

FRINGE

Cut a piece of cardboard 5" (12.5 cm) wide and 7½" (19 cm) long. Wind the yarn loosely and evenly lengthwise around the cardboard until the card is filled, then cut across one end; repeat as needed.

Hold together three strands of yarn; fold in half. With **wrong** side facing and using a crochet hook, draw the folded end up through a space and pull the loose ends through the folded end *(Fig. 1a)*; draw the knot up tightly *(Fig. 1b)*. Repeat in each ch-1 sp across short ends of afghan.
Lay flat on a hard surface and trim the ends.

Fig. 1a

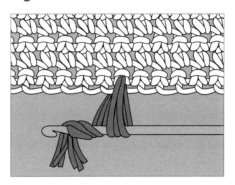

Fig. 1b

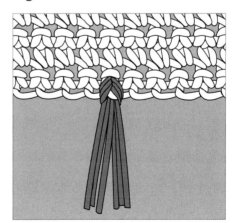

Yarn Information

The models in this leaflet were made using medium weight yarn. Any brand of yarn may be used. It is best to refer to the yardage/meters when determining how many balls or skeins to purchase. Remember, to achieve the same look, it is the weight of yarn that is important, not the brand of yarn.

For your convenience, listed below are the specific yarns used to create our photography models.

MULBERRY RIPPLE
Caron® Simply Soft® Eco
#0032 Plum Perfect

BLUE SEAGULL FANTASY
Caron® Simply Soft®
#9712 Soft Blue

BLUEBERRY DIAMONDS
Caron® Simply Soft® Eco
#0023 Blueberry Mist

LILAC MOSAIC
Caron® Simply Soft® Eco
#0028 Lilac Bud

PEACH OPPOSITES ATTRACT
Caron® Simply Soft®
#9737 Light Country Peach

PINK BUTTERFLY
Caron® Simply Soft®
#9719 Soft Pink

GREY SIMPLY SQUARES
Caron® Simply Soft®
#9742 Grey Heather

YELLOW SPRINGTIME
Caron® Simply Soft®
#0017 Lemon

Meet Michele Mireau

Years ago, Michele Mireau found a filet crochet pattern for an afghan. It was so easy and fast to do that she finished the afghan in just two days.

Michele says, "That was when I thought, 'I can do this!' I had so many ideas for afghans! I bought some graph paper and started designing. I made afghans for everyone I knew, using pictures of their children, pets, cars – shamrocks for my Irish friends – just about anything you can imagine.

"I live in Wisconsin, and I find that designing and crochet are the best way to spend the long winters here. I've been in the restaurant business most of my life and I look forward to retirement so I will have more time to design and to spend with my seven grandchildren.

"I love the ease of making my filet crochet afghan designs and watching their designs appear. They are very easy and can be crocheted in as little as fourteen hours. I'm passionate about these patterns, and I'm so pleased to be able to share a few with you!"

We have made every effort to ensure that these instructions
are accurate and complete. We cannot, however, be responsible for human error,
typographical mistakes, or variations in individual work.

Production Team:
Technical Writer/Editor - Joan Beebe, Jean Guirguis,
and Peggy Greig;
Editorial Writer - Susan McManus Johnson;
Senior Graphic Artist - Lora Puls;
Graphic Artist - Dave Pope;
Creative Art Director - Katherine Laughlin;
Photo Stylist - Sondra Daniel;
and Photographer - Ken West